AF862465

MY OWN MONEY MECHANIC

Shifting Gears for a Money Makeover You Can Live With

by Deb Schmitz
The Women's Money Mechanic
host of WomensMoneyMakeover.com

Published by Vision Run
305 Portsmouth Rd.
Knoxville TN 37909
visionrun.com

Copyright © 2011 by Deb Schmitz

ISBN 978-0-9826098-5-9

All rights reserved. No part of this book may be reproduced or transmitted in any form or by any means, electronic or mechanical, including photocopying, recording or by any information storage and retrieval system, without the written permission of the author or publisher, except for the inclusion of brief quotations in a review or article, when credit to the book, publisher, and order information are included in the review or article.

Cover and text design by Debbie Patrick, Vision Run.com
Photography by Brett Garvey, GarveyPhoto.com

Printed in the United States.

Praises for
My Own Money Mechanic:
Shifting Gears for a Money Makeover You Can Live With

Deb's writing style is engaging as well as informative. She gives valuable financial advice and makes planning easy to understand for everyone. I love her title—because she is a true Money Mechanic!

—Jennifer Alexander

Midday Host *WJXB-FM B97.5*

I thought I knew most of what I needed to know financially, but found information, and ways of looking at my money differently from this book, and so will you. Deb has poured so much of herself into "My Own Money Mechanic," and her passion is contagious. I highly recommend it for all women, and those who love them.

—Amelia Crotwell

Attorney-at-Law *Elder Law of East Tennessee*

Deb Schmitz has touched the heart of what women (and men) need to know about responsibly managing their financial affairs. Moreover, she has done so in an engaging and entertaining style, so that experienced and inexperienced alike can develop a plan to reach their dreams. Well done.

—Howard Sampsell

Vice President *AAA of East Tennessee*

Deb Schmitz has a passion for helping women take control over their finances! It's her mission in life. What sets her apart from all the other financial folks out there is that she has your financial well-being as her number one concern. That's refreshing. My Own Money Mechanic *is a must-read, especially if you've been avoiding looking at your long term financial health. Once you read it, I'd also urge you to talk to Deb one-on-one and let her take you to the next level. Working with Deb will give you the peace of mind to know that your future and your retirement are protected.*

—Denise Hedges

Business BreakThrough Institute .com

I am a man, an active investor and consummate saver for over 45 years and I found Deb Schmitz's book engaging, filled with insights and timely reminders of fundamental money management principles. Although it is written for women, I think most men would find it personally useful and helpful for the women in their lives, especially daughters. I believe it is so useful that my two daughters-in-law (one a psychologist in private practice and the other a finance major and stock broker) will each receive a copy. I hope they share it with their husbands!

—Thomas W. Osborn III, Ph.D.

Retired Research Fellow Victor Mills Society, P&G

Deb has a particular expertise in working with women who are not well-versed in planning and handling their finances. She can explain options and acts as a financial advocate in ways that save women money and financial worry. Deb's dedication to her clients is outstanding.

—Sue Painter

Confident Marketer .com

Acknowledgements

I want to thank and acknowledge my husband, Herb Helseth, who has been behind me throughout this process;

My Mom and Dad, who raised me with amazing ethics;

My brothers and sisters, whom I love dearly, for giving me the support I needed over the years;

Lillian Sims, a colleague in Cincinnati, who was the first person who told me I would be writing a book;

Sue Painter, "The Confident Marketer," who coached me to see the big picture and took me to David Neagle to be laser coached. It changed what I was doing, and really pushed me to write this book;

Debbie Patrick, Vision Run Publishing, who helped me put the words on paper;

Denise Hedges, Business Breakthrough Institute, my business coach, who has helped me through so much of my internal head trash, and introduced me to the Law of Attraction;

Fabienne Fredrickson, "Client Attraction" and all the "Goldies" I've interacted with. Fabienne's Mindset Retreats and her step by step approach are so valuable to me;

and finally, to all of the wonderful women who have the courage to face the process of making over their financial futures.

My hat is off to you all.

Dedication

This book is dedicated to my Dad,
Thomas C. Schmitz, (1930 - 2009)
You were my cheerleader—always telling
me how proud you were. It showed on your
face. You are telling me still,
but in a different way, and I miss seeing the
message on your face.

Your loving daughter

FOREWORD

Too often as women, we fail to take care of ourselves, as we look after our children, spouses, our work and the community at large. Not only do we fail to take care of ourselves, but many of us don't know the first thing about our finances and live in a state of what I call "avoidance and denial" around our money issues.

This was me too, many years ago. I'd started my own business out of my teeny tiny apartment in New York City and threw myself head first into growing it and getting clients, to the detriment of everything else, and although I was single and eventually became successful, I had a secret lurking... My unopened bills all lived in supermarket shopping bags that I kept under my bed, I was several years late on my taxes and because I wasn't paying my bills on time (including my rent!) the credit card companies were calling almost daily, and the eviction notices starting being taped to the front door of my apartment, for all to see.

I was in my late twenties/early thirties and not taking personal responsibility for my finances, and this unfortunately hurt me for years. What I realized is that although my actions weren't ideal, this wasn't my fault. I was behaving this way because I simply didn't know the first thing about how to handle my money and finances. I'd never been taught how to manage my spending and savings, didn't know the first thing about insurance or other ways of protecting myself against unforeseen circumstances and how to save for the future. And I believe I'm not the only woman who hasn't been given a full curriculum on money management.

But, one day, after it seemed like I had hit rock bottom, I acknowledged that no good would come out of continuing this "avoidance and denial" around the state of my finances.

So, I decided to take a no-excuses approach to changing my outlook and my behaviors around money, and starting taking personal responsibility for everything that had to do with my finances. I reached out to professionals who could teach me the intricacies of the process, how best to do things and started getting organized. I made it a priority to pay my bills (and rent) on time. I wrote down my dreams and goals and took consistent action toward reaching them. Within a few months, I was paying down my credit cards, getting help around my business bookkeeping, filing and paying back taxes and I was saving money for the first time in my life.

For me, it all started with speaking the truth about my situation. Once I got "real" about my circumstances, I was able to give myself a Money Makeover, and change the course of my life for good. Because what I've realized along the way is that The Universe (or whatever you prefer to call your creator) doesn't give you more of what you can't already handle. And once you get your own Money Makeover, you make room for more money to come into your life. That was my situation and because I've transformed my relationship with money using some of the same principles expertly detailed in this book, I was able to turn my business into a multiple 7-figure business and have created a life I love. This would never have happened upon a weak financial foundation.

And Oh, how I wish I had this book in my hands during my transition from "avoidance and denial" to taking "personal responsibility"! What's brilliant about the book in your hands is that Deb Schmitz simply asks us to get real and get clear on where we are exactly, taking into effect the realities of "real life." In sharing her own experiences, trials and tribulations, and eventual success, she allows us as readers to feel like we too can do this, when we're shown exactly how.

Deb doesn't talk down to us, but rather, joyfully brings us along this Money Makeover path, with surprising facts and most importantly, a step-by-step, very detailed and supremely actionable plan that is easy to follow. Deb is a powerful voice advocating for women in the area of financial planning, protection, and just plain encouraging us to take full responsibility for ourselves. It's akin to the stewardess on an airline flight telling us to put on our own oxygen masks first, so we're then in a position to help others.

So listen well to her wisdom, enjoy her stories and learn how to take the necessary steps to fund and fulfill your dreams, and help those you love to do the same. Most importantly, take action, big bold action on what's recommended in these pages. This will change the course of your life because, whether you realize it or not, money touches every single part of our lives.

Remember, it's not where you start, but where you're going that counts. Take the first step…

Fabienne Fredrickson

Founder of *ClientAttraction.com*

CONTENTS

Hire a Good Mechanic

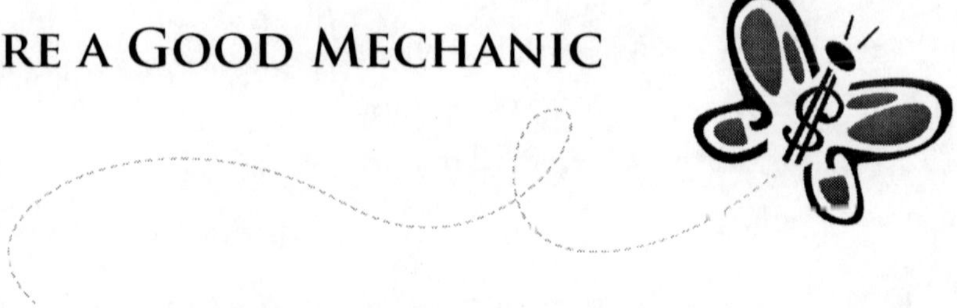

> *Money usually represents so much more than dollars and cents. It is tied up with our deepest emotional need for love, power, security, independence, control, self-worth.*
>
> – Olivia Melon

Motorized transportation comes in all shapes and sizes—there are motorcycles and mopeds, of course, and cars that range from hybrids and Mini Coopers to Hummers and mobile-home-sized RVs. From minuscule to monstrous, one thing they have in common is that they *all* need gas and, sooner or later, a good mechanic to keep them running.

It's essentially the same with your money: Some of us have small amounts, others quite a lot, but nearly everyone needs help with the "mechanics" of money's maintenance, growth, protection and management.

That's where I come in. Think of me as your money mechanic. I like to say that there's never too little and it's never too late to manage your money better. In fact, the earlier you start, the better, and that typically means you don't have a lot to work with in the beginning.

That's the fun part. Unfortunately, many people, especially women, don't think money management, planning or investing can be fun. Maybe that goes back to our culture, when we were told that girls don't like math or that boys don't like smart girls. It's a shame that society gave us those messages, but surely we've moved beyond that point now.

Ah, but unlike cars, which take a good bit more of your money than you'd like, money – when properly cared for – can transport you toward your dreams.
Deb Schmitz

Today, we're old enough and wise enough to realize we can re-invent ourselves *and* our thinking to work for us. Today, we don't have to let anything hold us back from being smart, capable, responsible women. If that sounds a little daunting, relax. I'm a great money mechanic, and I'll be right here to guide you through a complete "Money Makeover", one step at a time. We'll start our Money Makeover by looking at the broad picture.

The truth is that, according to a 2002 US Census study, 90 percent of women will be completely on their own, financially speaking, at some point in their lives. We typically out-live our spouses, and the divorce rate is skyrocketing, so whether it comes through death, divorce, or simply staying single, we women in particular need to know how to invest, save and protect our financial assets. Remember that financial assets are not just money. Assets are your house, car, your ability to bring in income to pay for things you need, including health care. Those assets should be able to take care of you when you are gone too. Don't let your family be burdened with trying to figure out what you wanted and having to pay for your funeral. You want to make things as painless and uncomplicated as possible.

I'm one who knows—I've lived through most of the available scenarios. My first marriage ended in divorce, I stayed single for quite some time before finding my wonderful soul mate, my husband, Herb. I've been through the retirement process and built our dream home, and I am still working (by choice). In addition, I watched my mother-in-law go from a very independent widow to being totally debilitated by a stroke, and I've watched and helped my mother through the adjustment of being widowed after a lifetime of marriage and raising five kids.

For these and other reasons, I feel uniquely qualified from the School of Life, as well as from my educational endeavors, to be your guide and money mechanic. In no time at all, we'll have your financial engine road worthy and running at top speed.

There's a special place in my heart for women when it comes to dealing with their money, because of my own experiences. That's why I went into the field of financial services. I'd spent a number of years in corporate America, in research and development with Procter & Gamble, known to most of us as simply P&G.

When I took an early retirement, I thought I understood finances more than most. Everyone used to come to me after P&G benefit meetings and ask, "What did that mean?" and I was able to explain it. Retirement, though, was a biggie and I just needed a little help knowing what to do with it. I'd received a nice package, and my husband and I were moving to Tennessee, building our new dream home. More than ever, it was a time I wanted to make smart money decisions.

Typical of my background in research, I began by doing my homework. I researched what various financial planners offered and attended numerous lunches, sales pitches and seminars. My biggest realization was that in all of these seminars, it seemed as though everyone said the same thing: "Give me all your money, I'm the best at figuring what you should do with yours." So I was at somewhat of a loss. I wondered, as you might be, how do you pick someone? What questions do you ask? How do you know whom to trust?

In my research to find the answers, I discovered how much I didn't know about what was offered or how to evaluate the many products and options on the market, and also how blatantly biased many of the planners and salespeople turned out to be!

For instance, I was the one with the retirement funds, yet in our meetings everyone seemed to direct their comments, advice and attention to my husband. Had I not been as strong-willed as I am, I would have been intimidated. As it was, I felt I'd been dismissed, shut out of the traditional "boys club," as if what they were suggesting was too big for little old me to understand properly, so they'd talk to my husband. Oh, boy, did they have it all wrong! In the first place, I've spent my entire life in fields dominated by men without feeling one little bit of intimidation or hesitation, and I've earned the respect of co-workers and supervisors alike along the way.

The other thing I've learned is the value of a "gut check." And my gut was going crazy, setting off all kinds of alarms. These people were not interested in me, they were interested in my money and making a sale based on what they had to offer, not necessarily what Herb and I needed.

> *A woman born during the baby boom will likely be widowed by age 67 and remain a widow for 15 years or longer.*
>
> **Dr. Nancy Daly**

It was that whole uncomfortable experience that led me to my new career in financial services—and my passion for helping women find their footing in this area. I often work with couples and find that women do very well at the day-to-day management of money. They often are the ones managing the household budget, balancing the checkbook and paying the routine bills. But when it comes to long-term planning and investments, they usually defer to their husbands.

That puts us in a dangerously vulnerable position when our husbands have gone; as I said, we tend to out-live them, and divorce sometimes happens. On top of that, the ugly truth of the matter is that most men don't know how to deal with long-term planning and investment. And I hate to bring up old stereotypes, but really, men are not known for their ability to ask for help or directions. Nagging them to make a doctor's appointment comes to mind. Whether or not they know or admit it, they need the help of a trusted advisor, and (this is where you come in) the support of their spouses in making the right decisions. Sometimes, without a little push, procrastination sets in, leaving you both without. By the time you need the benefit of long-range planning, it can be too late for some of the easy options.

So you can see I am passionate about people and their financial safety nets. You should insist on that from any financial advisor whose services you engage. If they're only interested in the money, they're not likely to have your best interests at heart. You need someone who not only has the qualifications necessary, but who will also look at your unique situation and determine what is best for you. Cookie-cutter solutions just don't cut it.

In the chapters ahead, you'll find both overviews and details about life situations and how to approach and prepare for them. While you don't have to read each chapter in order, I do encourage you to read them all, even if you think they may not apply to you right now. After all, you don't know what you don't know —but with an open mind, it's pretty easy to learn.

When I was at P&G, I didn't think I needed more insurance protection than the life insurance the company offered. I was completely wrong. (Read the chapter on *Diagnostics* beginning on page 37, to find out more.) There may be areas of your finances in which you are equally unprepared or lacking in knowledge. But I've made it easy for you to run a full road check, financially speaking.

As you explore this book, you'll find hope and insight, as well as courage and commitment to take your financial steering wheel in hand to make sure you're headed in the right direction. Then you can step on the gas or apply the brakes as necessary for a safe, secure future for yourself and your loved ones.

For more information, you can also visit my website, ***WomensMoneyMakeover.com*** for the latest developments, and to find out more. $

> *Married women with children under the age of 15 carry the heaviest workload of any group, about 77 hours per week.*
>
> **UN Human Development Report, Women in Diversity, Wow Facts, Business Women's Network, 2002**

Starting Out: Are You Stuck in the Family Car?

I have yet to hear a man ask for advice on how to combine marriage and a career.

– Gloria Steinem

Our families are a mixed bag when it comes to money—whether you love or hate the way "they" did it, the lessons you learned by watching your parents or extended family form some early and powerful ideas about how to handle money. And if you need to adjust your thinking, it helps to consider how you came to the conclusions and behaviors you have now.

Think of how you all piled into the family car when you were a child. It may have been a van, sedan or an SUV (or even a station wagon, if you're of a certain age), but it was typically large and practical for your family. You may have loved it or hated it, but it got the whole family on the road and off to your chosen destination. Still, you had no real choice.

Your ideas about money are very much like that family car. They were established before you got here, and you had no choice in the matter. As a child, you had no vote in either the choice of transportation or destination. But it's different now.

It may be time—or well past time—to step out of the "family car" of ideas about money and get your own ride. Maybe something a bit more updated and stylish, something more practical and with better mileage than what you grew up with, because times have changed. What used to be great advice… may or may not be good advice now.

For example, I remember when 401(k) plans first came out. They weren't nearly as good as the "Cadillac" pension plans put aside for you completely through company contributions, but if you were going to have to provide your own retirement savings, they were great vehicles because they used pre-tax dollars. You could get a tax break today by saving for tomorrow. Say you earned $30,000, but because you put $2,000 in your 401(k), you paid tax on only $28,000, and you had that little extra put away for retirement too. It was a double benefit. If your company matched your contribution (also without your having to pay tax on it), that was like getting "free" money.

Admittedly, that was a long time ago. The belief back then was twofold: In retirement, you'd be in a lower tax bracket. You would pay less in taxes when you took the money out vs. the taxes you would have had to pay while you were still working.

You wouldn't need as much income in retirement – the rule of thumb was that you would only need 70 percent of your working income to live on in retirement.

Well, welcome to the future, ladies, because now that we've lived 25 or so more years, we're realizing that a few things have changed. First, taxes vary so much that we're most likely *not* in a lower tax bracket whether we're "retired" or not.

Second, while inflation overall has not been too bad, the rising cost of healthcare, has outpaced inflation. This translates to people *needing the same income in retirement that they needed when they were working*. Third, Roth IRAs have come along—helping you grow your money tax -free.

In light of "then and now," try to catch your assumptions about what is "good" when dealing with your finances and look at them with fresh new eyes. Look at your spending habits. Why do you spend what you do, where you do? How are your spending habits different from, say, your best friend's? How are they the same as your parents' or your siblings'? Then look at your saving habits, or lack thereof. Think about the logic, attitudes and history you have of buying, saving and investing. Then ask yourself where those ideas came from, and are they still true or useful.

As you work through the next section, keep re-examining your ideas and actions regarding money to see whether they still serve you well today. Remember, you don't have to stay in that old family car of your parents' attitudes and actions regarding money. Just because they didn't save or invest doesn't mean you can't learn how to do it and become quite successful. By the same token, if your parents managed money well and

> *Now is no time to think of what you do not have, but rather think of what you can do with what there is.*
>
> **Ernest Hemingway**

you just can't get the hang of it, keep reading because it's time for a new money car for you. TODAY!

Don't Run Out of Gas!

The whole intent of this trip through life is not to run out of gas, i.e., money. You know you have to keep filling up your gas tank on a regular basis in order to get from point A to point B. This book is designed to help you through the short trips (day-to-day management) and the long trips (retirement and not outliving your money).

The first thing to do is to determine where you are, which in financial terms means knowing what you have, what you are spending and where you are spending it. Think about all the new GPS technology that is out there to help us find our way on the road. It even talks to us. Too bad we don't have one to help us with our money. Imagine purchasing a $6 cup of coffee instead of a $1 cup of java, and when you hand the cashier the money, the GPS would say "Please return to your highlighted path." If you made a big purchase item when you really couldn't afford it, the GPS would say "Make a U-turn as soon as possible." But even if we had such a device, it would still need two pieces of information: where you are, and where you want to go. It does not care about where you've been. So let's dump all of that heavy luggage, turn a new page and figure out where you are! $

TRACKING OUR ROUTE

> Beware of little expenses. A small leak will sink a great ship.
>
> – Ben Franklin

Now as I mentioned earlier, women are often fine with the day-to-day management of financial resources. If you are, great. But if that is troublesome, if there is too much month left at the end of your money or if you feel you would, could or should do it better, you are ready to start at the beginning. You need to keep a record of what you are doing or you won't know how to fix it. I hear groans already. You have to do this, but only for a month. YOU MUST KEEP TRACK OF YOUR SPENDING. All of it. Devise a system that works for you. I find it interesting that you, as a customer, need to actually ask for receipts at many places, so keep that in mind. Make it as painless as possible.

Here are some ideas:

- Keep a plastic pencil box in your car to keep all of your receipts.

- For families or single moms, try keeping track of what is for you and what is for your kids. For instance, when you eat out, jot it down on the receipt. It doesn't have to be perfect or exact; round numbers work great.

- Have a certain section in your purse where you put your receipts.

- Tally your receipts at the end of each week or even each day. It will seem overwhelming if you wait until the end of the month.

- Keep receipts for cash, credit and debit transactions, and carry a small spiral notebook in your purse to jot down spending for which you can't get a receipt – for a vending machine purchase, for example.

Once you've done this for a month, you'll have a wealth of information at your fingertips. This is a typical month, and this is really what you spend; you have the proof right in front of you.

One woman I talked to couldn't believe that she was spending $240 a week on groceries and cleaning supplies! So the first step after you've done this write-down-every-penny-all-month-long exercise is to notice where you spent your money. Is it where you thought it was going? Does it reflect your real priorities? What surprises you?

> *Nearly half of all women do not know how much money they will need for retirement. 56% plan to rely on their husband, inheritance, or a stock market windfall to support them in old age.*
>
> **2002 survey commissioned by Million Dollar Roundtable, an association of insurance and financial professionals**

Next, categorize each expenditure, into either fixed or discretionary spending. Fixed expenses are those you must spend: rent or mortgage, utilities, insurance payments, etc. Discretionary expenses are more voluntary in nature. While you have to eat, food is in this category because you have a great deal of discretion about where and what you eat, and therefore how much you spend. Other discretionary expenses include entertainment, dry cleaning, cat food and litter, gas for your car and so forth.

Third, set up "even billing" wherever you can. Most utility companies offer level billing, and you may find other opportunities for that as well. Doing this helps you turn variable expenses into "fixed" expenses.

Fourth, look over your list for ways to save or cut down, i.e., turn off the lights when you're not in the room, as it will help lower your utility bill. Eat in more than you eat out.

Now you're ready to set up a spending plan based on real numbers and your own personal priorities. For some people, going out to eat is essential. For others, essential is getting their hair done each week. A good spending plan is built to help you with short-term as well as long-term goals. If you *can* do without that $6 Starbucks two times a week, wouldn't you rather have $624 by the end of the year that went into savings and you received

Small Spending Changes Add Up to Big Savings

	Monthly	Annual	10 Years
Buy regular coffee instead of lattes/cappuccinos	$1.75 $3.50 $5.25	$21.00 $42.00 $63.00	$320.15 $640.31 $960.46
Rent a video instead of going to the movies	$4.00 $8.00 $12.00	$48.00 $96.00 $144.00	$731.78 $1,463.56 $2,195.35
Prepare lunch at home instead of dining out	$6.50 $13.00 $19.50	$78.00 $156.00 $234.00	$1,189.14 $2,378.29 $3,567.44
Borrow books from the library instead of buying them	$20.00 $40.00 $60.00	$240.00 $480.00 $720.00	$3,658.92 $7,317.84 $10,976.76
Exercise at home instead of at the gym	$50.00	$600.00	$9,147.30
Don't purchase that extra pair of shoes/sneakers *per year*	n/a n/a n/a	$100.00 $200.00 $300.00	$1,523.94 $3,047.88 $4,573.65

20 YEARS	30 YEARS	40 YEARS	50 YEARS
$1,030.78	$2,608.12	$6,109.26	$13,880.52
$2,061.57	$5,216.25	$12,218.52	$27,761.04
$3,092.35	$7,824.38	$18,327.79	$41,641.56
$2,356.08	$5,961.43	$13,964.03	$31,726.90
$4,712.16	$11,922.87	$27,928.06	$63,453.81
$7,068.24	$17,884.31	$41,892.09	$95,180.72
$3,828.63	$9,687.33	$22,691.55	$51,556.22
$7,657.26	$19,374.67	$45,383.10	$103,112.45
$11,485.89	$29,062.00	$68,074.65	$154,668.68
$11,780.40	$29,807.18	$69,820.15	$158,634.37
$23,560.81	$59,614.37	$139,640.13	$317,269.09
$35,341.22	$89,421.56	$209,460.46	$475,903.64
$29,451.02	$74,517.97	$174,550.39	$396,586.37
$4,906.54	$12,414.69	$29,080.09	$66,071.28
$9,813.08	$24,829.36	$58,160.19	$132,142.57
$14,725.51	$37,258.98	$87,275.19	$198,293.18

with an 8% rate of return? See the chart on pages 26-27 for some real eye-opening examples of how small savings can add up over time.

By knowing what you're spending, you can begin to control it to the point that you have money to set aside for emergencies, investments, savings and insurance.

In knowing where you are, to recap the thoughts of the first chapter, it is a good idea to be mindful of some of your thoughts about money. Were you brought up in the generation where girls were discouraged from going to college because it would be a waste of money? The logic was that, after all, you would just find a husband, get married and have kids and then all that education and money would go to waste. I was. Not that I listened to it completely (obviously), but I know that it affected me nonetheless. $

> *The average monthly Social Security check for a woman over 65 is $697, which is $207 less than a man.*
>
> **Social Security Administration**

Dangerous Curves Ahead: The Road to Great Credit

(or, Making Credit Work For and Not Against You)

If we could sell our experiences for what they've cost us, we'd all be millionaires.

– Abigail Van Buren

It's a modern world, and while none of us likes the idea of credit cards and all the mischief that can be made with credit scores, interest rates and possible debt, they are also convenient and required to operate in the real world.

There are a number of new laws governing your credit and credit cards in recent years that make it more important than ever for you to know your credit scores, and keep up with your credit reports — these are two different steps.

Like creating your spending plan, you can't regulate your spending if you don't know where you are. Credit is the same song, different verse. You must know where your creditors or potential lenders think you are in order to know where you stand, and plan wisely.

As the credit market tightens, driven partly by those new laws, it also changes the decisions you might be making about paying off your credit cards. This is another instance of "conventional wisdom" advice needing a new evaluation.

There was a time when if you had a high-interest credit card, you would have been told by all the experts to pay off the balance with your savings, because your savings were earning less than the credit card or cards were costing you.

Today, if you do that you may not be able to get the credit availability back, and without your savings, you'd be left in a very vulnerable position. So while paying down your credit cards is always a good idea, make sure you don't drain your savings to do it.

The first step to great credit is knowing exactly what is in your credit report. People talk about "your credit report" as if it's a single report, but it's actually three different reports, one each from the three credit reporting bureaus: Experian, TransUnion, and Equifax. Information is constantly being added to each report, and so any report you get is just a "snapshot" of a moving target. But it's a start.

From your credit report, your FICO score or credit score is generated, and again, you have three different scores because each one is generated from a different report. In theory, the credit score is a way of summarizing a consumer's credit-worthiness on a somewhat scientific and non-biased basis.

So the first thing to do in your investigation into your own credit standing is to know your score. These were once more closely guarded secrets than your medical records, but this is the information age, and you can get your own score now on the internet. Go to the website www.MyFico.com. You will have to register with a credit card, but after you feel you've gotten appropriate value, you can cancel their monthly fee service at any time. In the meantime, you've gotten your score. Next, you'll want to get copies of the credit reports that generated your credit scores. Again, the internet is your friend. Go to AnnualCreditReport.com, and get your report from all three reporting bureaus once a year, for free.

> *Bankruptcy cases filed in federal courts for fiscal year 2010, the 12-month period ending September 30, totaled 1,596,355, up 13.8 percent over total FY 2009 bankruptcy filings, according to statistics released today by the Administrative Office of the*
>
> **U.S. Courts.**
> **Bankruptcyaction.com**

Now you know what your lenders know. You may have heard horror stories, as I have, about the frequency of discrepancies on your credit report. Personally, I've never found a mistake on any of mine, so know that not all credit reports are bad or inaccurate.

If you do find things that are wrong, you need to contact the bureaus that have the wrong information in order to correct it. If you find the information is accurate but unflattering, there are things you can to do correct that too.

Your final credit score is affected by many things, like credit-to-debt ratio, (that is, how much credit you have used vs. how much is still available to you) your job stability, how often you have moved, and other things, but don't worry about most of that. You have to live your life.

The two most important things you can do to affect your credit score are:

- Make sure you never miss a due date on your payments, and ...
- Don't use all the credit that's available to you. In fact, use less than half of the credit that's available to you.

If you do those two things, you will eventually have a great credit score, regardless of what your reports and scores are saying now. As I said, they are moving targets, so by making on-time payments and not using too much of your credit, you can tip the scales in your favor.

Do this credit check exercise of checking your reports and scores annually, and you'll protect your good credit. If there are mistakes in your reports, the sooner you address them, the easier it will be to fix them. If too much time has passed, all your records that would have proven the mistake will be gone. So put this on your list of things to take care of, just like your annual physical, income tax filing, and so forth.

Bumps in the Road

What do you do if you're already "in over your head"? First, keep it in perspective. It's not the end of the world, but it does need to be addressed. Now that you have the facts about your score, make a list of all your credit card balances, minimum payments, and interest rates.

Next, total the minimum monthly payments. Compare that total to the total amount you can apply each month toward paying off your debt. Now pick one of your credit cards to focus on at a time. Make minimum payments on all the others, and pay all of your extra budget toward that one card until you get it paid off or paid down to a comfortable level. Then focus on the next card or debt on the list, and so forth.

This gives you more of a sense of accomplishment and progress than spreading the extra payments over all your creditors. Some people recommend focusing on your smallest debt first so that you get that boost of confidence from paying it off fast. Others recommend you start with your highest interest rate debt first. It really doesn't matter. Just start somewhere, and focus on moving forward. You can do this.

Driving at a Reasonable Speed

Now why should you care about your credit reports and scores and so forth? For one thing, employers are increasingly checking job applicants' credit reports. Thirteen percent of companies conduct credit checks on all job applicants, according to the Society for Human Resource Management. This use of credit isn't new; the federal government has been conducting credit checks since the 1950's. But it's getting a lot more attention because of the economic downturn.

Sooner or later, you will need credit. It may be for a house or a car, or just a new sofa or car repair. When you apply for credit, your credit reports and FICO scores determine what kind of loan you can get, what type of interest rate, and even if you can get credit at all. So be prepared before you need it, by making sure your credit is always in good shape.

How much credit you're comfortable with is a highly personal decision, based on your income, spending habits and other factors. Many financial gurus talk about credit as if it was a one-size-fits-all issue. And like clothing that makes the same promise, it just doesn't typically fit. There is no one answer for everyone, except perhaps to not buy more than you can pay for. Just because using credit makes it easier to say yes to "want" purchases.

Personally, I like using credit cards because it is easy to keep track of what we spend. The key is paying them off every month. So the answer to how, when, where and how much credit you use is up to you. But my advice is to make that a deliberate decision, part of your planning, and part of your budget. That's the best way to have credit work for you, and not against you.

> *The average American household has 14.27 credit cards and carries an average outstanding credit card balance of $7,034.*
>
> **US News and World Report, 6/17/02**

In addition, you should make sure you have at least one credit card in your name only. When you get married, your credit report stays the same, but your spouse's accounts, or any accounts for which you are authorized to sign, are added to your report. But there are no "joint" credit scores. You and your spouse each have your own scores and histories. When you go to get a loan or a mortgage, the lender will look at all three reports and scores for both of you before they make a decision. That's why it's so good to know the facts in advance, so you're not surprised or caught off-guard.

As I said earlier, I've been lucky regarding my credit reports in that I've never had to correct errors. I have a friend who was not nearly so fortunate. Her first name was the same as her husband's first wife's name. And she (the first wife) had credit problems. Even though the reports are supposed to be filed by social security numbers, which are different for each individual, my friend's credit report was constantly confused or mingled with that of her "predecessor." So even if you're married—keep up with your own credit report.

Remember, too, that not all debt is "bad." Mortgages and school loans can be considered "good debt," while credit cards are considered bad debt if you can't pay them off with ease. $

Diagnostics: Protecting Yourself

The future belongs to those who believe in the beauty of their dream.

– Eleanor Roosevelt

By this time you may be realizing you need some professional assistance and advice in sorting out "best practice" financial habits and plans from the ones that are not quite so supportive. That's why I designed the Money Makeover.

Have you ever been to a mechanic who wasn't very good at diagnosing a mechanical problem? You go into the shop thinking you have a problem with your fan belt. The first thing they ask is, "What's wrong?" You say what's happening and that you think it may be the fan belt. They're more than happy to replace it—even if it doesn't need replacing because the real problem is your water pump. After a few times in the shop over the same problem, you may think you have a lemon when what you really need is a new mechanic.

That's why diagnostics (as well as good mechanics) are so important. You can't fix anything properly unless you know what's truly wrong—or right—in the first place. Regardless of all the computerized everything under the hoods of today's modern cars, a really good mechanic can just *listen* carefully to an engine as it runs and have a pretty good idea of what's going on under there. That's why a good mechanic is so valuable.

It's virtually the same with managing your money. You wouldn't think to change the fan belt yourself and neither should you make all your financial decisions alone—but where do you start? An inexperienced or self-focused financial advisor will make a strong sales case that you need the products and services on which he or she will make the most money. Maybe you do, and maybe you don't. But a really good financial advisor will first listen. Carefully. Then he/she will ask questions, and listen some more. Only after getting an accurate picture of your life and circumstances can an advisor give you a full and accurate diagnosis and recommendation.

Now that we've talked a little, it's time to do some diagnostic work on the financial protection (insurance) you have in place in your own life. Here are some questions—I like to call them MPG, for "My Protection Guide." They are questions you need to ask yourself, to make sure you have the right protection in place:

MPG (My Protection Guide)

Health Insurance

- What happens to your coverage if you lose your job?
- What happens to your coverage when you or your spouse retire before age 65?
- If one spouse has coverage through work, do you know what happens to coverage for the non-employed spouse, if something happens to the employee?
- If there is a divorce before retirement, what happens to the coverage?
- If there is a divorce after retirement, what happens to the coverage?

Disability Insurance

- Do you and your spouse have it?
- How long does it last?
- How much will it pay you?
- When will it start to pay you?

Long-Term-Care Insurance

- Do you and your spouse have it?
- How long does it last?
- How much will it pay you?
- When will it start to pay you?
- Does it have a cost-of-living increase? Simple or compounded?

Loss of Life

- Do you and your spouse have life insurance?
- How much is it for?
- How long does it last?
- Who is the beneficiary?
- Where is the policy?

We'll go into detail further in the book about why these are good questions to be answered before you start on your journey, but once you get the answers to these you are well on your way. One word of caution about the questions, though: Don't be surprised if you get some strange reactions from people you are in relationships with when you start asking them. When I gave this list to some friends of mine, their husbands felt threatened. One thought his wife wanted a divorce. Another thought his wife was going to knock him off when she asked how much life insurance he had! *But these are important things to know* no matter how uncomfortable you feel asking about them. If you are in the same generation or general era as I am, asking your parents these questions is even more difficult. They never talked about money. They had probably been taught by their parents that it was their "secret."

Armed with the answers to your questions above, you need to talk to your "mechanic"—a qualified independent financial advisor—to determine the best plan to put in place to protect your future. Remember, there's never too little money to work with, and it's never too late to plan.

If your financial advisor doesn't feel the same way—for instance, if he charges high fees just for consultation or requires some high minimum estate value to talk to you about your investments—run! Find another financial advisor who will care about *you* first, and then your money.

As we talked about when I mentioned the family car, whether you believe it or not you carry a money blueprint with you from your upbringing. Think about all the sayings we have been fed during our youth. *Money doesn't grow on trees, Do you think I'm made of money?* and *Money is the root of all evil.* You may have embraced these ideas or rebelled against them, but

Women spend 40% more time than men researching a fund before they invest, yet 70% of women investors feel they are too strapped for time to deal with Financing. Only 56% of men feel the same way.

Women's Financial Network and Women's Economic Status Report

they influenced your thinking one way or another. And a pattern revealed is a pattern with much less power over you.

Since this is a book and not an interactive strategic planning session, you're going to have to do some of the diagnostic work, but I'll be with you, helping to point out the importance of each part as we go along. Then you'll be able to know if that knocking sound you keep hearing in your financial engine needs further attention. $

30,000 Mile Checkup

> There isn't a part of our lives that money doesn't touch. It affects our relationships, the way we go about our everyday activity, our ability to make dreams reality, everything.
>
> – Suze Orman

The first stop, foundational to your financial road-worthiness, is insurance—all types of insurance—auto, home, health, life, disability and long-term care. (The definition of insurance is *financial protection against loss or harm.*) The law requires that we have it for our automobiles and the banks require homeowners insurance for a mortgage, but it's far more important for overall protection in other areas of life. There are many different types of insurance, and they can be confusing, I know. But it is essential that you get this general category right – just as essential as it is to change the oil in your car.

You wouldn't think of buying a home without also purchasing homeowners insurance, yet you and the people in your life are far more valuable than any property you'll ever own. Don't take it for granted that everything will remain the same. As I have learned and watched others learn painfully, nothing lasts forever.

In essence, the right insurance coverage involves a series of quality-of-life decisions that you make for yourself and your loved ones in advance of a need. And to do nothing is a choice that can leave yourself and your family vulnerable to disaster at worst, and heartache at the least.

Life Insurance

When I was younger and working for P&G, I had life insurance equal to my salary through the company. I thought that was enough, especially since it would pay double my annual salary if I died in a work-related accident. I had no children and my husband had a good job, so he could continue to make the house payments—no problem, right?

Then life started to make some turns. While these changes were not in my plans, in retrospect, they were not all that unpredictable either, had I been more forward-thinking in my personal planning.

My husband was downsized, making me the main breadwinner. How would he survive now if something happened to me? To complicate things a little more, P&G was downsizing too, and offering those of us with significant seniority a great early retirement package that included healthcare coverage for both of us until we reached 65.

> *Most retirement plans require five years of active employment to qualify to receive benefits. The median length to stay at a job for women is 3.8 years vs. 5.1 years for men. As a result, less than one-third of women working in the private sector qualified for retirement benefits in 1998.*
>
> **Women's Institute for a Secure Retirement**

It rocked our world a little, but we had been planning for retirement in a few more years anyway, and had already built our dream home in East Tennessee. The only problem was that it had a higher mortgage than the one we'd had when we were both still working. We decided to move South earlier than we had originally planned, bringing us back down to just one mortgage, even if it was a little high. Still no major problems, right? We'd both get jobs when we got settled, and we had our newly expanded nest egg to fall back on too.

After our move, I ended up having double knee replacements, and during the course of my recovery decided to take a life/health insurance class to get licensed. As a committed lifetime learner, it had always interested me.

As eye-opening experiences go, this one was stunning. I had it all backwards. Did I mention that I was 49 and my husband was 55 and still a smoker? We needed life insurance and the price for purchasing it was now astronomical. Unlike our earlier situation, if something happened to either of us, the other would have a hard time keeping up with the mortgage and the bills.

Learn from my mistakes

The time to buy life insurance is when you are young and healthy and don't see the need for it. The industry rule of thumb is 8 to 10 times your salary, which can be misleading at times. If you are the main or only bread winner and you have a mortgage and small children, it may need to be much more than that. I like to use the question: How much money do you need per month? For every $100,000 of insurance you can achieve $500 of income per month. For instance, if you need $1000/month of income per month, you need $200,000 of life insurance.

…I also had a small variable life insurance policy that I bought because I liked the concept. I could be my own bank and borrow money from the cash value and pay myself back at a really low interest rate. It did serve me well. I used some of the cash to put a down payment on a car. Little did I know, I understood only half of it. These types of policies are great, but they are very complex. I was lucky—my friend that sold me the policy realized I thought I understood it but didn't really. He made sure that the policy would not lapse or as I say "go belly-up" before I died. And like my friend Jane's story that follows, I had no other life insurance outside of my work. The fact is, women outlive men, statistically speaking—by six years. In my case, my husband is already six years my senior, so I am likely to outlive him by at least 12 years. If you are a woman, you need life insurance on your partner if you have one, and for yourself if you have anyone who depends on you—or you don't want to burden your heirs with the expenses of a funeral.

My friend "Jane" is a perfect example. She was a dear friend of mine who worked with me at P&G for more than 20 years. She ended up dying of cancer at age 47. Both she and her husband worked with me, and they had three teenaged children. One was in college, while the other two were still in high school. At that time, Jane and her husband were like me in that they had insurance only through work. We used to joke about how "Uncle Procter took care of us." But not this time; Jane's death came way too early. You can imagine how I felt as I listened to her son at the service and then read in the paper that a fund was being set up for her children's education. I am certain this was the last thing she would have wanted—to have to depend on others to pay for her kids' education. If they had done some early planning, the insurance would have been very inexpensive—they were young when they started their family. Also, when they were younger, they were both very healthy.

54% of women are more likely to accumulate 30 pairs of shoes before accumulating $30,00 in retirement savings.

Oppenheimer Funds survey, 2001

The older you get, the more you are at risk for having an illness—one of those being adult-onset diabetes. Once you get diabetes, you are basically uninsurable and if you do get insurance, you pay a high premium. This includes health insurance, long-term-care insurance *and* life insurance. The only way you may be insurable is through a group plan such as those offered by large or mid-sized employers. Although as this book is being written, Congress is working to change this. It may be years before the changes trickle down to your own ability to acquire the insurance you need.

Again, in my own family, my father died after an extended illness, just as I had started writing this book. Despite the fact that he and my mother were not wealthy, they knew the value of life insurance. They both had policies and I as the financial caretaker knew about them too. Those two facts made it so simple and easy at a time when we were all under tremendous stress. I had a check from the insurance company within two weeks of my dad's death, which we needed and used for the funeral and other expenses. It also gave peace of mind to my mother and my siblings as well.

> *The average woman's balance in a 401(k) account is a little more than half of the average man's... On average, only 27% of a couple's retirement need will be covered by savings, 401 (k), IRAs and similar plans.*
>
> **Fidelity Investments report, Building Future, March, 2001**

It almost didn't happen like that, though. Just a few years earlier, as I had changed careers and began to understand the whole insurance industry, my parents received a letter from their insurance company that they didn't understand – sound familiar? My dad had a type of universal life policy, a hybrid between whole and term life insurance that was popular in the 1980s. His policy had cash value, but also an end date when he would "age out" and have no more insurance. Because my parents had taken out a loan against the policy over 10 years ago and didn't understand what that meant, the age-out date was earlier, in fact, just around the corner. To make things worse, they had purchased the policy from my second cousin, who had not kept in touch with them. We will talk about that a bit later. I had to jump through a number of hoops with the insurer but was able to save his policy. Good thing, too, because by that time my dad was uninsurable. Without saving this policy he already had, he would not have qualified to buy another one.

It's a simple way to prevent a personal family disaster such as what happened to my friend Jane and her family.

OK, I'm an unabashed convert—much of insurance is owned by the richest people in America, because it is a very efficient wealth transfer tool. The death benefit goes to the heirs free of income tax. Your children may be grown, your grandchildren or other loved ones may not depend on you—but with life insurance, you could change the course of their lives long after you're gone.

If you're the one who may be left behind, one of the most sobering statistics I know is that 24 percent of widows and widowers go through their spouse's death benefits in just *two months*. That's not even enough time to grieve much less make a whole new financial plan for your life. The bottom line is that life insurance is one of the most loving and protective things you can do for your family.

You also need to look into long-term-care insurance as well as disability insurance (no, they are not the same thing).

Long-term-care insurance (LTC) will protect and provide for you if you are unable to live independently. It will pay for assisted living, nursing care at home or a skilled nursing facility without first forcing you to liquidate your entire estate, as Medicaid does.

Needing long-term care without long-term-care insurance is the biggest risk to your retirement nest egg. Until you go through it with a family

The number of women more than 100 years old will double in the next 10 years.

US Administration on Aging

member, I think it is tough to wrap your mind around. According to AARP, 79 percent of those expecting to need nursing home care incorrectly believe Medicare would foot the bill, but the fact is Medicare typically takes care of only 2 percent of the costs nationwide. Moreover, Medicare takes care of very specific needs only. I think this is because many people get Medicare and Medicaid mixed up. To put it simply, Medi*care* is what you are eligible for when you reach age 65. It covers your basic health care needs. Medic*aid* is a different program that activates only when you have become a ward of the state. By this I mean that a contract between you and the state is basically set up. The state agrees to pay for your room, board and medicine in exchange for your income. Your choice may be limited because at this point only facilities that have Medicaid-approved beds will take you. Each state has their own asset and income levels for eligibility. Currently, in the states of Ohio and Tennessee, you must have less than $1,500 of assets to go on Medicaid.

To "hide" assets by giving them away or re-titling them to friends or family is looked upon as fraud. It's really very sad, and at that point, when you need full-time care and can't pay for it, there are no easy answers.

My mother-in-law is a great example of a near-miss for this kind of heartache. Her name was Katherine and she lived in Florida. Her husband had pre-deceased her so she had been single for years but she was quite active and healthy for her age. She still lived in her own home, frequently went bowling and swimming and was very active in her church. But we received a call from her neighbor in the spring of 1993. Katherine had experienced a stroke. The neighbor who called us hadn't been able to get in contact with her, so she called 911. The emergency medical technicians (EMT's) found Katherine in her chair at home. They told us the stroke had probably occurred the day before. We rushed from Ohio to Florida.

Katherine did not have a power of attorney for finances or health care, or a living will, although she did have a will. My husband was her only child. Luckily, Katherine was still cognizant when we arrived. Instead of going directly to the hospital to see her, we had to get to the attorney immediately and have all the papers drawn up. The day after she signed them, she lost the use of her hand and her speech. My husband's name was already on her checking account, but that wouldn't have helped a whole lot. If he had not been able to get those papers signed, by law he wouldn't have been allowed to do much to help her. (We'll talk more about this in the chapter on Your Owners Manual, beginning on page 77.)

After her hospital stay, we had to put Katherine in a nursing home, first in Florida, then Ohio. We had to sell her home and car and use most of her assets to pay for the nursing home. Because she had no long-term-care insurance and far more than $1,500 in assets, she would be required to pay for her own care. That is, my husband, who now was able to manage her finances, was required to use them to pay thousands per month for her care. Only when her assets were depleted would Medicaid pay anything. This is what is called "spending down assets."

We looked long and hard for a nursing home that was both private pay and Medicaid approved so we wouldn't have to move her when the time came to go to Medicaid. My husband had just started the process for

Medicaid when Katherine passed away in October of 1995. For her care we had gone through over $200,000 in 2½ years.

This is not what Katherine wanted to do with her house and her assets. She wanted her son to have them, but she kept putting things off. Can you imagine if things had been different? If Katherine's husband were still alive, all their money would have still been used to take care of Katherine. There would have been nothing left to take care of him.

In this case, long-term care insurance would have been the ideal solution. However, the solution is not the same for every situation. There are life insurance policies with LTC riders or options that can be used for critical illness and terminal illness; these options are "living benefits," meaning that you don't have to die to use the insurance policy.

I am finding that the insurance industry is like any other industry. When the consumer wants something else, they will come up with a solution. Recently some new products have been introduced. The insurance companies heard consumers say they didn't want to be paying thousands of dollars a year for something they may not ever need (although the odds are against that). Now there are annuities that can be purchased that can be used for long-term health-care needs. If you do not use the money, it goes to your heirs. A nice win-win situation.

I have a friend who is a family counselor and she's quick to point out the emotional benefits that LTC insurance has on individuals. When the decision time comes to move to from your home to assisted living or retirement places, many different emotions can result. Some of these are natural reactions to change. If a spouse is widowed, moving anywhere can feel like leaving the loved one behind, where there were so many memories of a lifetime shared.

But if you have planned ahead, there are no added concerns for financial welfare. You will not be a burden on your children. There is also more confidence because you made the choice of where to be and you know what to expect. It still may not be ideal—all of us want to live long and healthy lives in our own homes, but with LTC insurance, it is far easier to deal with less than ideal circumstances.

Being afraid of change can either prompt you into action by planning appropriately or it can keep you from doing anything. There may be the grieving of leaving a house, apartment or residence that held many life memories. There are higher risks of developing depression, particularly if you are not prepared for the change. Concerns about paying for the care, dipping into money designated for children or grandchildren or for care of a spouse can have a devastating effect on self-esteem and give a sense of losing of control over one's life. Pre-planning allows you to feel more in control of your life and responsible for decisions made concerning your care.

Disability insurance

Disability Insurance is one of the most misunderstood insurance coverages available. It is very complex, but I want to touch on it and share with you a very basic understanding, *because it is the most important insurance to have, and most people do not have it.*

Disability insurance is the insurance that will pay your bills when you cannot work. When you have been disabled, not only do you not get paid, but if you have been contributing to your 401(k) for retirement through

> *Women are a dominant financial force. In 2002, they purchased more than 50% of all new vehicles, constituted 40% of all business travelers, influenced 80% of all travel, and owned 38% of all U.S. businesses, contributing $1.6 trillion to the national economy.*
>
> **American Woman Road and Travel**

your employer, that will stop also. Many people do not take that into account when they are thinking about these types of coverages.

Whether it is you or your spouse who loses income through illness, accident or injury that leads to disability, it can be a difficult change to manage. A close relative of mine I'll call Jim had been self-employed for years as a home-improvement specialist. Most self-employed individuals do not have disability insurance because they feel it is too expensive, as was the case with Jim. At age 52 he had a major heart attack, followed by multiple heart attacks in a six-month period. Now he has a defibrillator and pacemaker in his chest and hasn't been able to work since April 2007. In fact, he will not be able to work again. Even though his wife is employed, their house payment, cars and other financial obligations were based on having both incomes. His loss of health touched the family on a number of levels. There was the grief associated with the loss of employment, loss of physical capabilities, mental capabilities and relationships that were forever changed, all in addition to the new financial hardships.

I can tell you after watching their very personal struggles that, in addition to the damage to self-esteem and feelings of worthlessness, disability can have a huge impact on your feelings of being able to care for yourself. Concerns over caring for your family, spouse or other dependents can be overwhelming and detrimental to your recovery. Pre-planning allows you to feel more in control despite situations that may seem very much beyond your control.

> *The average adult of 65 or older spends nearly one-fifth of her annual income, or $2,400 on health care. Prescription drugs account for the single largest expense for older adults.*
>
> **AARP**

So, back to your own money makeover—what do you look for? How do you choose a good policy? With disability insurance in particular—you get what you pay for. You need to read the fine print. There are so many variables. Key questions to ask are:

- How much does it pay?
- For how long?
- When does it start?
- Am I insured for not being able to work in my own occupation or only if I can no longer work in any occupation, i.e., sweeping floors?

Many people believe that they can get disability through the government. Yes, this is true, however, plan on being denied at least the first two times you submit paperwork. There are so many fraudulent cases submitted that unless the government knows you are serious enough to hire an attorney, you most likely will not qualify. Again, Jim knows this firsthand. It took him almost three years to the day of his first heart attack to get approved for permanent disability. He hired an attorney and one of his brothers even works for Social Security—the government entity that handles SSD (Social Security Disability).

Many employers offer disability insurance, yet people don't take advantage of it because they don't understand it. In general, women's coverage is more expensive because they live longer. If you are self-employed, many insurance brokers can provide good coverage. Yes, it can be expensive compared with other insurances, but you are insuring your greatest asset, your ability to earn income. According to insurance industry statistics, the odds of becoming disabled are greater than dying, having your car totaled or your house burn down. $

Life, Liberty and the Open Road

Long-term care is a women's issue. Women often deplete their assets financially and emotionally caring for elderly parents and spouses.

– Deb Schmitz

Buying insurance is a little like picking a car—do your research, and read the contract carefully. There can be a world of difference in your coverage. You want a good policy from a good company, one that will be there when you need it. There are financial ratings for the insurance industry, typically from independent organizations. AM Best is one of the best known. They issue ratings, or grades, for an insurer's financial stability that range from A+++ to S. Anything lower than a B+ is considered a financially vulnerable insurer.

Any insurance, be it health, disability, or long—or short-term care, becomes more expensive as you get older. Past a certain age, insurance may no longer be available for you to purchase at all, so timing is everything. If you are married and have health insurance through your spouse's employer and you become widowed, you may find yourself also without health insurance coverage, and you may by that time be uninsurable.

I remember as a young adult that many of my friends had life insurance policies their parents had purchased for them when they were children. Most of them dropped the policies when they had to start paying the premiums themselves. What a huge mistake! A life insurance policy is one of the greatest gifts a parent or grandparent can give a child. When the insured is a minor, there is no physical exam involved, and you can add riders that enable you to increase the death benefit without having to go through underwriting (the process the insurance company uses to determine if you are worth the risk – which usually requires a physical). That is an outstanding benefit, because should any health issue arise later in life, it may be the *only* way to get any additional insurance.

When I think of all my friends or acquaintances whose children were diagnosed with leukemia, diabetes, Crohn's disease and other illnesses... well what a blessing to already have insurance in place that can grow with your needs.

Now I have several good friends in the life insurance business. Each had purchased policies for their children at a young age. By the time their kids were in their twenties, the cash value had grown so they could use the money for college, or as a down payment on their first home. The stipulation was that they could not drop it. I am not saying to make this a first priority as where to spend your money. I like to mention it because I think it is a great gift for a grandparent to give. Much better than a savings bond or clothing that the child will outgrow. And most people don't think about it.

Another reason to have life insurance on your children is the mere fact of burial expenses. If something tragic ever happened, you would be distraught enough without adding the financial burden of funeral expenses.

There are more policies now that you can purchase for burial/funeral expenses. They start as low as a $2000 death benefit to pay for funeral expenses and can be purchased from age 40 or so up to age 85. Again, they have minimal underwriting and may be great for seniors who do not have a "bucket of money" set aside to pay for burial expenses and don't want to burden their children with the expense. The cost of an "average" funeral can run as high as $6,000 to $10,000. Again, the earlier you plan for it, the better.

You can also pre-pay for your funeral. This is usually done through a funeral home. They use life insurance in the same way – to fund your funeral expenses. You buy the insurance through them. This can be very comforting to seniors and their children – just be sure there is something in writing that deals with what happens if the funeral home is not there when you die.

The point is, you never know what the future may hold, but you can plan well to be protected, almost no matter what.

Some general definitions are helpful here. You need to know the options and what they mean, although every policy is different, so read and question carefully before you buy!

There is a "pecking order" as far as expense is concerned.

In General

Most expensive to least expensive

Whole life → Variable → Universal → Term

Whole life insurance - you actually own the insurance and it can increase in cash value that can either increase the death benefit or you can get a "loan" against the policy. It costs more, but there are plans that allow you to purchase term insurance and convert a portion of the coverage to whole life insurance over time. This is how you bite small chunks off.

Variable - your premiums are invested in mutual funds and may lose or gain in value, beyond the cost of the insurance. If you "over fund" it, you can be your own bank account. I used mine for car down payments. Once you understand it and use it correctly, it's amazing how it works, although it is very complex.

Universal - essentially, "term for life" insurance, in which you pay for it as long as you live. You may be able to build some cash value with some carriers.

Term insurance - you are "renting" insurance for a specific period (term) of time. It is inexpensive by comparison. You buy for a set amount of time, say, 10 or 20 years, and pay the same premium throughout the life of the policy. When it ends, so does your insurance, and your payments. You have no cash value in the policy.

One additional word of caution: Be very careful about the ads you see on TV and in senior publications such as AARP. They promote the fact that they accept anyone, and they do, but they may pay no benefits until after the coverage has been in place for a certain time. Do you have a crystal ball? $

Destinations, Dreams or Diversions?

> If all the cars in the United States were placed end-to-end, it would probably be Labor Day weekend.
>
> —Doug Larson

Before you can map out a trip, you must first know where you want to go, of course. That's where the "armchair traveler" comes in, the dreamy travel brochures, video travel catalogs and imagining yourself on the beach sipping a cool beverage, climbing the high sierras or some other grand adventure.

It's the same way in life and financial journeys, and in fact, is just ahead of the place where life's goals and money's goals intersect. To know your goals, you've got to know your dreams, you have to know where you want to go, who you want to be, what you want to do in life. Then you can plan your life and financial goals to support your dreams.

If you haven't let yourself dream in a while, it's time to re-acquaint yourself with the process. There was a television commercial that started off showing a 30-something-year-old while the voice-over says "*Remember when you were 5 years old and anything was possible? Happy fifth birthday.*" You may not have to go back quite that far, but that's the idea.

> *In 2002, more than one in eighteen women in the United States was a business owner. 73% of all women-owned businesses are based in the home.*
>
> **US Census Bureau and Center for Women's Business Research**

Think first of what you'd want to do, in every area of your life, if money, time and health were not considerations. This is not the time for practicality, self-editing or second-guessing. Give all those parts of your brain the day off. This is the time for serious dreaming. If the sky really were the limit, what would you do?

Write it all down and keep brainstorming until you've remembered everything you ever thought about wanting to do, everywhere you wanted to go with your life. Then think of some new dreams you can get excited about and write them down too. If you find your well of dreams a little dry and rusty from neglect, turn the questions around. What circumstances would you *never* want to find yourself in? What do you just hate? What is most important to prevent?

Again, we're just dreaming here, like calisthenics for the brain (you remember those jumping jacks and other exercises from gym class long ago, right?). It's playing, yes, but with a greater purpose.

There's another silly commercial that comes to mind, the one where someone slaps his forehead and says with astonished regret, "*Wow, I could've had a V-8!*" You've probably never regretted what juice you chose, but when it comes to planning your life rather than your meal, I think it would be really tragic to come to the end, and feel, "Oh if I'd only thought about it a little more I could have... done something more." It happens to people all the time, but it doesn't have to.

American poet and abolitionist John Greenleaf Whittier once said, "Of all sad songs of tongue or pen, the saddest of these, '*It might have been*'." So don't let this opportunity pass you by. Put this book down right now and start getting in touch with your dreams. Go ahead, write them down. No limits.

Now that you've got your dreams on paper, the more practical side of your brain has probably kicked in with, "You can't do all that," or the more popular and sarcastic, "That'll never happen." And you'd be right about some of it. But without the dreaming, you can't do the sorting, selecting what you want to do from what you really don't want, or don't want any more.

Sometimes we let everyday urgency overshadow the important things in life. The dreaming exercise lets you get back in touch with what's truly important and necessary. You can't be an astronaut *and* a brain surgeon. And if you're either of those, you aren't likely to experience hitchhiking around Europe, although you may see Europe in a more luxurious way if you choose.

Now is the time for getting practical, editing, evaluating and prioritizing your dreams as you set your goals. Remember, for goals to be achievable, they need to be SMART, that is:

Specific (exactly what do you want to accomplish?)

Measurable (how will you know when it's finished?)

Achievable (push yourself a little here, it shouldn't be too easy)

Realistic (alas, world peace may have to remain a dream)

Time-specific (a deadline for when you will have achieved this goal)

What does all this dreaming about life have to do with the sometimes dry and dusty mechanics of money management? It's simple. Your dreams and goals are the motivations that enable you to press on toward your financial goals. Then your finances enable or disable your larger life dreams and visions.

As you look at your list of dreams, you'll find some are more important to you than others. For myself, I've found that spending time with my family is truly important, but sometimes easy to let slip out of my schedule with work and daily distractions. And while I always dreamed of going to Singapore, I won't be devastated if I don't.

Using our analogy of planning a road trip, you'll find that some of your dreams are not really worthy of turning into goals, because you no longer want them or because they're more diversionary in nature instead of real, primary destinations you want to reach. (For example, in my twenties I wanted to join a parachuting club, but now in my fifties, not so much.)

Prioritizing Your Goals

Like a good relationship or a good traveling companion, a great set of long-term goals are going to be with you for awhile, so it's a good idea to "date" before you make a big commitment. Try turning each dream that is a potential goal into a SMART goal. What would it look like? How would you make that happen? Then look over the entire list, for balance, clarity and my famous "gut check." Is there anything you've left out? For instance, are all your goals about work, to the point that if you embrace them all, there would be no time left for family? You may need to go back and set some goals regarding your relationships. Then look again at your list of potential goals. Which ones will really make the cut? Which ones are the most important of the most important?

With this advance planning, your own financial advisor—almost like a good travel agent—can help you see what it would take financially to help support those goals. That enables you to ground your goals in reality and is also a good time for you to evaluate them one final time before making a long-term commitment.

Your Roadside Emergency Kit

If you're happily married, that's wonderful. But please don't skip this section. You never know when you may need to recall the information that follows, for yourself, or for a friend. Having been there myself, I can tell you that in the middle of a marriage breaking up, it's very difficult if not impossible to think straight. I'm told it's also hard to think when your life partner is seriously ill or dying. Don't make it harder on yourself than it has to be. Like any good emergency training, the time to gain preparatory facts is long before tragedy strikes.

In one small sense, death or divorce can be somewhat analogous to losing your car to an accident—it can happen fast, demand all your attention as you try to avoid it, and have lasting effects that you needed to have prepared

> *I am a marvelous housekeeper. Every time I leave a man, I keep his house.*
>
> **Zsa Zsa Gabor**

for in advance. And just as if you're going to be without your car for a time, it helps to know the bus or subway routes and have correct change. In other words, (need I say it again?) you need to be prepared.

I remember my own divorce. It was exhausting. All my mental and emotional energy was tied up in trying to make the relationship work, and up until the very moment when I realized I couldn't — I kept thinking we'd get through it. Even when we were separated, I was too distracted and tired of thinking about the marriage to begin to look around and make a plan for myself. There wasn't a time when I said to myself, "Gee this might not work out, I'd better think about some kind of plan for financial shelter should the worst thing happen." So when the worst did happen, like many others, I was unprepared.

I had married young, to a guy I'd met in my college chemistry class. We had an adventurous first year of marriage. Our apartment was hit by the tornado that swept through Cincinnati in 1974. The building was condemned due to the damage, so we had to move—*fast*. That was in April. Then my father-in-law died in September of that same year, the day after my 21st birthday celebration. That was followed by my grandfather's death in October. There was a time when I would have told you that if our marriage had survived all that, we could weather any other storms that might come along. But we didn't.

We were married for six years and finally decided to go our separate ways. People who have not experienced divorce think that's the easy way out. Not by a long shot. Anyone who has gone through it will tell you just the opposite. Divorce is one of the hardest decisions I've ever had to make—and we didn't even have children!

You've heard it said that the only two "sure" things in life are death and taxes. Actually, there are three sure things: death, taxes, and *change*.The degree of change in your life when divorce happens is almost unfathomable. Your friends change, where you live (and how you live) changes—if not physically, then at least emotionally. Your finances change. Traditions change. No wonder it's so stressful, before, during and afterward. (Incidentally, many of those changes—friends, finance, traditions and more—also happen if you become widowed.)

When I worked up the nerve to tell my family I was getting a divorce, they thought I was crazy—and they wanted me to see a counselor. Little did they know that we had been seeing a counselor already, but to no avail. Before the divorce, we had been separated for almost two years. During that time, I didn't get myself prepared. Instead, I just learned that the grass wasn't greener on the other side. So while I knew what I didn't want (a divorce), I still didn't know what I *did* want. We got back together after those two years, and decided to build a house. It was a better rationale than having a baby, like some couples do. But our logic was the same: We were thinking that something new and different would change things, or change us.

The house, which was modeled after the house I grew up in, ended up being a nightmare with the contractor. In fact, the company offered to buy it back from us because so many things had gone wrong. But no, we had it in our heads this was going to fix everything. We lived in the house together for only one year. When we split, even as emotionally attached as I was to the house, I was the one who moved out.

We tried to sell it, but the housing market was very slow. Over a year later, we switched places. During this time, we agreed that whenever we did sell the house, we would split the proceeds. In the meantime, our split and conversations were pretty amicable.

I was going to get a roommate and take care of the house, which I did. One day I was working in the yard, and a co-worker of my now ex-husband stopped by. He said he was interested in buying the house. By this time, I was pretty settled and was enjoying the house, so I said no, I was going to keep it. My ex-husband called me that night, excited that I was keeping the house – saying that one of us should have it after all the trouble we went through with the builder.

Later that year I met my wonderful soul mate, Herb, the guy I would eventually marry. Problem was – he had a house too. So we decided that he would sell his house and buy my husband out of his share of mine.

By that time, the housing market had gone down even further. When I had it appraised, the house was worth less than when we originally had it on the market a year or two before. As we had chatted that day in the yard, my ex-husband's co-worker had mentioned a higher figure than what it was appraised for now, when I finally did want to sell it.

That was when my formerly reasonable and agreeable 'ex' now wanted half of the amount that had been casually offered by his co-worker, rather than half the true value of the house. Ladies, hear me loud and clear: Hindsight is 20/20. Foresight is fairly clear if you work with professionals to prepare. But right-in-the-moment sight, well, that's not always so great. I should have just let my ex have the house, but emotions got in the way—I got attached to the house and essentially paid for it twice.

For many women I work with, the new realities of single again are a rude awakening, because from the eye of their marital storm, the single road ahead hadn't looked all that daunting. For some, in fact, it looked much more peaceful! Others feel trapped in relationships—even abusive ones—because of their lack of ability to be able to provide for themselves financially. It's a tough place to be, but there is help available. I encourage everyone to consult with a financial advisor you trust, who can help you think clearly through the financial issues and take advantage of help that is available to plan the rest of your life. Remember, there's never too little, and it's never too late to create a financial plan.

I have talked to so many newly or nearly divorced women who have had to, as advice columnist Ann Landers was fond of saying, *wake up and smell the coffee*. No question about it, divorce is devastating, emotionally, financially and every other way possible, especially if there are children involved. So many women have thought, "No he'd never…" or simply assumed that both parties would be civil adults in settling their joint affairs in order to prepare for separate futures. Others don't even know the full extent of what the marital assets are, much less where they might be hidden. No matter how amicable your divorce, go over every account and benefit. I do not want to harbor mistrust in any marriage, but it is your right to know what is yours. Do not just trust what someone tells you. Understand it for yourself. Case in point—I had a woman come to me for advice as her divorce was starting. She handed me a very organized spreadsheet with all of the assets listed. I started asking her questions about each of the assets and she didn't know how the amounts were determined. I then asked who made up the spreadsheet, and she told me her husband had provided it. Again, she trusted her husband—and I am not saying that is wrong, but my gut was twisting, knowing that she was clueless about how and where these assets were determined. Her husband had even placed a value on the house. When I suggested she have an appraisal done, she said no, she didn't want to rock the boat. There are too many of us that don't want to rock the boat! We need to – that boat is just as much a part of our lives as it is our spouse's.

You need to know your rights, because it isn't fair when marriages don't work out, and if you're naïve enough to think that his lawyer will encourage him (or vice versa) to do right by you, well, you're taking an extremely large risk with little chance of winning. If you lose, then it's doubly unfair.

The first thing to realize is that once you've decided to get a divorce, it becomes a business deal between your lawyers. Generally speaking, attorneys representing the wife will want to settle matters quickly, because there is a window of time during which the husband feels guilty for the failed relationship and they want to take advantage of that. Attorneys representing husbands, on the other hand, want to drag things out as long as possible. During this period when nothing is settled, the wife is typically very short of cash, particularly if the husband was the main breadwinner. Remember, these are merely strategies employed to get one's client the best possible outcome. This is a business negotiation, and as with any negotiation, forewarned is forearmed.

If it is in your best interest to decide matters rather quickly, you must know the facts way ahead of time. For instance, you might pay the day-to-day bills out of a household account, but your husband handles larger investments. Do you know what those investments are, where they are held, what balances you have? Many women don't, until it is way too late to easily find out.

> *Two-thirds of all divorces are initiated by women.*
>
> **American Law and Economics Review 2/1/2000**

Even the best marriages end because no one lives forever. A friend of my parents' is a perfect case in point. Her husband died at a fairly early age, and all she knew about his business was where they kept the key to the front door. She was tragically unprepared.

Statistically speaking, you will likely be responsible for yourself financially at some point in your life. Whether you ever face divorce or not, it's very important that even in the most blissful marriage, you maintain your own financial identity.

If your marriage is in trouble, it's doubly important, of course. In my experience, if a couple isn't communicating well enough to continue their marriage, they are definitely not communicating well about their finances. In fact, finances are named as one of the top stressors on a marriage and a primary reason for divorce. So if you learn to talk about your entire financial picture together, you're not only protecting yourself, but helping to preserve your marriage too. If you can do this well, you'll do other things in the marriage well, and that is a very good thing.

At least once or twice a year (and preferably more often than that) ask to see the investment accounts. Look at the statements, ask questions — not like a Spanish Inquisition, but generate some genuine interest in your joint financial affairs. I have a friend whose husband had been taking money out of his 401(k) and funding another account without her knowing it. He was planning the divorce. He had forged her signature for the withdrawals, because by law, the spouse has to co-sign withdrawals from any retirement account. When the divorce finally happened, neither she nor her divorce attorney asked for a backlog of 401(k) statements. Only the most recent one was shared—the one with no withdrawals.

Remember that if you ever do get a divorce, you are *both* responsible for all the debt incurred jointly during the marriage. No matter what it says in the divorce decree, if he ever defaults, you're on the hook for the full amount. Divorce courts don't have the legal authority to alter contracts entered into jointly by a married couple. Likewise, if you are widowed you are also responsible for all the marital debts, even though you no longer have his income to help pay them.

This is why it pays, no matter what your situation, to educate yourself about where things are, and what to expect, so that if accounts are suddenly smaller or otherwise amiss, you'll be aware of it. You'll also be prepared in case something happens to your spouse and you have to take over the savings and investment management as well.

Now if you do find yourself facing divorce, an important point to keep in mind is that *equitably* dividing your assets does not mean *equally* dividing your assets. Although this is changing for younger couples, the wife typically is the one with the lesser career and money-making potential, while the husband generates a larger sum. In addition, the wife typically has greater expenses involved in moving on, particularly if she has given up educational or career opportunities in order to raise children or care for family members. And there are overhead expenses beyond merely childcare and education.

Because women tend to move in and out of the job market, to take care of families, young children, aging parents and so forth, our retirement contributions suffer. And while we may be just as qualified and educated as men, we still earn on average, about 20 percent less.

Statistics show that men bounce back from divorce significantly more quickly than women. One sociologist who studied the economic effects of divorce in the late 1990s reported that women experience a 73 percent drop in their standard of living during the first year following divorce. Men, on the other hand, often fare better in terms of the financial effects of divorce. According to statistics, men enjoy a 42 percent rise in standard of living within the first year of divorce. This is especially true if the woman has been the homemaker during the marriage. It can be a time of incredible stress, and fear or anxiety as well. Few go into marriage thinking, "Oh well if it doesn't work out, we'll just get a divorce." Of course not. So it's safe to say you never thought you'd be faced with this situation. Accepting it, and that life is going to change dramatically because if it, is half the battle.

It's the women who stay stuck in denial and/or regret who have the most trouble moving on. So take time to grieve the losses, but also face facts, gather good counsel and focus on making a plan for your new life circumstances.

Once you're divorced, you'll probably no longer be covered by your spouse's health insurance, and you'll no longer be beneficiary of his life insurance either (as a rule) or his pension. So there are many things to think about and negotiate.

Emergency Kit Essentials

>1 – Try to be pragmatic in a divorce. Don't let emotions tie you to physical things – like houses.

>2 – Know what assets you have. Don't be the person that backs down. You are not being mean, aggressive, bitchy – whatever name they want to give you. You are entitled to half.

>3 – Know about employee benefits. His and yours. This includes health insurance, life insurance, disability insurance, retirement plans. $

The Scenic Route: Retirement and How to Get There in Style

> Men who have a pierced ear are better prepared for marriage. They've experience pain and bought jewelry.
>
> – Rita Rudner, comedienne

Too many of us spend most of our lives wishing large parts of them away. Have you ever noticed? It's more than questions of "Are we there yet?" and "When do we get there?" like anxious kids on a long trip. We're all subject to some version of the same dynamic throughout our lives. When we're very young, we look forward to getting old enough to go to school. But once we're there, it's not enough. In grade school, the cool kids are in the upper grades. They get to change classes. That's when life will be great. Then once we're a little older, it's when you get to drive then everything will be good. By then, having your own car is the big deal. Or a job. Or the next big promotion.

We're so focused on the future that we sometimes forget to enjoy the present, or forget to take the actions necessary to make that future reality the one we envisioned.

Retirement is like that. We dream of it, imagine it, fantasize about what it will be like. Yet too few of us get to live the dream.

As I've said, if you're a woman you have a certain number of factors stacked against you, and a more urgent need to overcome them. Remember: Ninety percent of women will be entirely responsible for their financial affairs at some point in their lives, generally due to death or divorce. In 2000, 40 percent of all women aged 65 or older were living alone, and 51 percent of those age 80 and older were living alone, according to AARP.

Yet we as women typically make less money, making it even more challenging to save for retirement or the proverbial rainy day. And the jobs we have offer fewer benefits such as retirement plans, too.

You may be part of the "sandwich generation," those still caring for their kids and taking on responsibilities for aging parents. The natural expectation might be that your children will care similarly for you, but don't count on it. Overall, families are less involved in caring for older generations—36 percent of us have grown children who live 100 miles away or more. As generations have evolved, have you noticed the difference in how we take care of older generations? My mom had her mom's sisters living with them. Now, your mother may live with you, but she has her own "apartment" in your home. There are assisted living places, aging in place is popular—where the home is modified and hired help comes in. Who knows what it will look like when we get to our eighties.

If you're planning on your husband's life insurance, remember that 25 percent of all widows go through the husband's death benefits in just two months.

Ideally, a woman of 40 should have more than $100,000 in savings and investments earmarked for retirement. But in fact, the average 40-year-old woman has only $7,000 saved, according to a Financial Literacy study. If you haven't gotten your retirement paid for, you're certainly not alone, but as everybody's grandma is fond of saying, there's no time like the present to get started.

For some of you, the task is a bit more urgent than for others, and the choices you make will be different depending on the stage of life you're in, your health, family situation and so forth. But the key is to look at the facts, make a commitment and take action—today—this one's a big deal. Like death and taxes, growing older and less able to generate income is a given for most of us.

Retirement may sound like something very far away, something to think about "later" if you're quite young. It comes up much sooner than you think and it is *so* much easier to have the future you imagined if you start early and develop good saving and investing habits.

Nowhere is the old cliché
"the early bird gets the worm"
more evident than for those who start early saving for retirement – even if you're not consistent.

Age 21 **$2,000** per year	**Starts Contributing** **Invests**	**Age 37** **$2,000** per year ***(until she retires at 67)***
Age 31 **$20,000**	**Stops Contributing** **Total Contributions**	**Age 67** ***(when retired)*** **$62,000**
Assumes an average 8%	**Annual Return**	**Assumes an average 8%**
$499,659	**Account Balance at Age 67**	**$246,691**

Saving for retirement is significantly different today than it was even a few years ago, and miles away from depending solely on the company pension and gold watch offered to our parents' and grandparents' generations.

The major facts influencing the change? People are living longer, meaning that retirement could last as long as 30 years (or more!) That takes a substantially larger nest egg to sustain. Without proper planning, "living too long," that is, outliving your money, could become a harsh reality.

Another major consideration in retirement planning is the rising cost of living. We don't have double-digit inflation like we did in the 1970s, but prices are steadily rising nonetheless. Even if you paid off your house, the cost of taxes, gas, utilities, food and healthcare continue to grow.

Unlike decades past, company pensions today are as rare as antique cars, and given the economy, equally unreliable. Defined Contribution plans have replaced Defined Benefit plans (the downsized edition of a pension), meaning that *you*—not the company—pay as you go for your own retirement, and your contributions are optional. Although, now some companies are requiring employees to put 5% percent away in a 401(k) or other retirement plan they offer.

Social Security is on increasingly shaky ground and may or may not be around when you retire. So whatever age you are, it's time to take the wheel yourself and start driving toward the future under your own power.

Let's take a look at the basic strategy for retirement planning: At the least, you want to be able to reduce your expenses and maximize your income or savings now so you'll have enough to last throughout your lifetime.

A common theme among women is to do as much as possible for their children. We take care of everyone else before we take care of ourselves. Retirement planning is where you have to be selfish. You need to save for retirement *before* you save for college for your kids. Once you have the retirement saving systematically under control, then and only then should you start saving for your children's' college. The thought process here is that you can always get a loan for college. You cannot get a loan for retirement. Another thing to think about: If you are not self-sufficient in retirement, you could be a burden on your children. It is much easier for an adult child to pay off a student loan than it is to take care of an elderly parent. So while it may sound counter-intuitive, save for your retirement before you pay for your children's college education. It's best for all of you in the long run.

And when you do reach retirement, you'll want to stretch your dollars as much as you can. One way to reduce your expenses during retirement is to have your home and cars paid off. With your housing taken care of, all you have to worry about will be your taxes, utilities and day-to-day expenses. This easily reduces your monthly expenses by 25 percent, although as I mentioned earlier, with the rising cost of healthcare, you really need the same income in retirement as you had while you were working.

There are a number of ways to make sure your mortgage is paid in full by the time you retire, including making mortgage payments every 4 weeks instead of monthly, giving you a 13th payment annually, which should be designated to go toward your principle, paying it down much more quickly. Make sure you check the terms of your loan, that there is no penalty for paying it off early.

Some people need the mortgage interest in retirement for tax reasons, but again that may change with new tax laws. That is why it is always a good idea to meet with professionals that you trust. Just as we talked about earlier, in the same way you don't want to be changing your own fan belt, neither should you rely on your own logic for tax advice. See a qualified professional who specializes in tax law—a CPA.

On the savings and investment side of retirement planning, your options read like a bowl of alphabet soup.

Individual Retirement Accounts, or IRAs, come in a variety of flavors now. These and similar accounts are essentially structured savings and investment plans designed to help you get to a successful retirement. I define that as having enough money to not work and not worry at the very least, and ideally, to also have enough money to get to do the things you'd really like to do. That may be travel or philanthropy or just playing golf every day or spend time with your grandkids.

The first step is to take a long, hard look at your expenses, income and lifestyle and set a goal for how much money you'll need for retirement. It's best to work with a trusted professional financial advisor for this.

Some of the terms you'll become familiar with are IRA, 401(k), 403(b), 457, profit sharing, ESOP, pension, SEP, SIMPLE. Most of the time, people just refer to these accounts as "my retirement" or "my IRA," when in fact each of these have special rules about how they are treated by the IRS. The ones defined by numbers come from the number designating the tax code that governs them. Here are a few things to keep in mind:

> *Women see themselves less likely to be risk takers than men. 31%of women label themselves conservative investors compared with 21.7% of men.*
>
> **Women's Financial Network**

- Your money *will* be taxed – either before you put it into an account or when you take it out.

- A Roth IRA is the one that is taxed before you put it in. It grows tax-free and (unlike a traditional IRA) you don't *have* to start taking distributions when you are 70½.

- Pensions are going by the wayside. These were typically with large corporations that guaranteed an income for the rest of your life. Most of these plans have been lumped into a category called Defined Benefit plans because the benefit is defined.

- Profit sharing and ESOP (employee stock ownership program) use company stock as the benefit.

- All the others are pre-tax dollars and will be taxed when you take the money out. The theory here is that you will likely be in a lower tax bracket when you're withdrawing your funds that when you put them in. As I mentioned earlier, this is not necessarily the case.

- SEP and SIMPLE IRAs are usually set up by self-employed people or those who work for small companies with no formal retirement plans – again based on the rules set up by the IRS.

Remember there are penalties for most withdrawals, if you take them out before age 59 ½, because they are designed to encourage and accelerate your retirement planning.

As you read the fine print on your options and discuss them with your advisor, remember the difference in pre-tax and after-tax dollars. Pre-tax dollars usually means money is paid into a retirement plan before taxes are taken out, reducing your taxable income right away, while after-tax dollars means the money you bring home in your paycheck, after the government has had its cut. Investing in a Roth IRA is an example of using after-tax dollars.

Pensions

If you (or your spouse) are lucky enough to have a pension, here is something to think about—but you need to think about it when you are still healthy. The concept is called "pension-max," meaning that usually when one has a pension and it comes time to retire, the company gives the retiree some choices. With one option, you get the highest dollar amount per month, but it leaves the spouse with nothing when the retiree dies. Most people pick the 50:50 choice, which gives you 50 percent while the retiree is alive and the spouse gets 50 percent when the retiree dies. But what if the non-retiree spouse dies first? The retiree is living on only 50 percent.

I'm going to go back to life insurance again—I told you I am a convert. If you both bought life insurance at an early age and converted it over time to make it permanent, you could take the maximum monthly amount from your pension, even if the non-retiree spouse dies first. If the retired spouse dies first, the remaining spouse has the life insurance proceeds to provide income. The surviving spouse could set up their own "pension."

> *One-third of all women would rather talk to their grandmothers about their love life than to a financial consultant about investing.*
>
> **Oppenheimer Funds survey, 2001**

The problem is, most people don't talk with anyone outside of their HR department at work regarding their pension or long-term planning. You need to be talking to someone like me early on in your life. I can't tell you how many times I have talked to people about this and they love the concept, but by then they have developed a health problem late in life and cannot get insurance. Others had life insurance and then cancelled it when they got to be 50 because the kids were gone and the house was close to being paid off.

"Nancy" experienced the worst case scenario on this. Her husband, Bill, worked nearly 50 years as a traveling salesman, and finally retired. In all his years of traveling, he'd never had so much as a fender-bender of an accident. Instead of taking a "lump sum" at retirement, they chose to get monthly income for (his) life, and were looking forward to "the best years of our lives." Just two weeks after he retired, he died tragically in an auto accident, the victim of a high-speed police chase in which he was an innocent bystander. But all the papers were signed, and there was nothing that could be done. As the widow, Nancy received nothing but a small death benefit from their life insurance policy held with the company. All the pension income ceased with Bill's death.

Please, please, please—if you bought life insurance *do not* blow off the salesperson when he or she calls for the annual review. Everyone says "They are just trying to sell me something else," but in reality it is this advocacy for you that makes this work. It is much easier to do this all in small steps than it is taking off big chunks. If you bought term insurance, ask about converting it to permanent insurance. And don't automatically drop it once the kids move out of the house. Remember my dad's story, as well as mine. (And before your appointment, be sure to read the chapters on Diagnostics, 30,000 Mile Check Up, and Life, Liberty and the Open Road. All will prepare you for your talk about insurance!) $

YOUR OWNER'S MANUAL

Live as if you were to die tomorrow. Learn as if you were to live forever.

– Mahatma Gandhi

Okay, hang in here with me, because I am going to go somewhere that no one likes to go. I say this because over 70 percent of you don't have them. I am referring to wills. The statistics are appalling regarding the number of people who die without them. Please don't be one of them. It makes a very difficult and stressful time even worse for your loved ones, as it is much harder for them to take care of things.

Many people say "I don't care, I'm not here" or "I don't have anything of value" or as my mother-in-law said "I don't have anything to worry about, my son will take care of it." This is faulty thinking. Without a will,

> *The average life expectancy for a woman in the united States is 80.2 years, and the average life expectancy for a man is 75.1 years.*
>
> **National Center for Health Statistics, 2006**

whatever you own individually—be it a lot or a little—can be distributed by the state, vs. the way you might want.

So *please, please* do not make it any more difficult for those that are left behind. This includes anyone – your family, lawyers and courts. This is especially important if you have children. Do you want the State to decide what happens to them? I do not know what the issue is with completing this one task. Maybe people don't like to think of death. What you're really doing is taking care of your loved ones after you're gone.

As the saying goes, "The two things in life you have to do are die and pay taxes." It's not a matter of "if" but a matter of "when" so don't go thinking you're the exception. If you could take a survey in heaven, I'm betting you'd find 98 percent of the people there thought they'd have more time on earth. So take care of it now, before it's too late. It's one of the most loving things you can do to protect your family.

Maybe you think it is too expensive. A simple will can be drawn up for about $500 for a couple. This usually includes two or three other important documents – a living will, durable power of attorney for healthcare, and durable power of attorney for your finances.

Now after I've said do it, do it, do it now, I have to add a word of caution: If you are inclined to be a do-it-yourselfer, be very careful. Every state is different. It is worth the couple hundred dollars to get it done right the first time. Yes, the will may be written in "legalese," but this is how the attorney lets the court know in no uncertain terms exactly what you have explained to him or her that you want to have done. It can be as general or as specific as you'd like. The will needs to be witnessed and notarized. Do-it-yourselfers often miss this.

I help people talk about this difficult subject before they go to an attorney. It helps to have thought things through before you go. Have your questions written down and have a list of all your "stuff" and who owns it. This is where people get hung up thinking they don't need a will. I hear this all the time—"I don't have an *estate*." *You* may not dignify your collective assets by calling them that, but the State does and will place a value on it. Dying without a will is called "Intestate". When you die and own property individually without a beneficiary or pay on death designations, the state will divide the assets among the heirs according to state statutes. This may not be anything like the way you would want it to be. The state will look to grandchildren, parents, siblings, nieces and nephews, aunts and uncles. When you determine and direct in advance how you want your assets distributed, that's called a will. Your estate is your assets. That can mean a house, car, savings, checking, and Aunt Nancy's wing chair. You do not have to be rich to have an estate. But to be sure your loved ones will have your possessions and not more burdens after you've gone, you *must* have a will. Just do it.

You might imagine, and rightly so, that I preach about the necessity of wills quite often. And as I watch people deal with the responsibility, I've noticed an amusing pattern (amusing from my standpoint, anyway.) For whatever reason, a lot of people seem to finally make a commitment to do their wills just before leaving for a deluxe vacation. With all the planning, packing and shopping, they add even more pressure to themselves by deciding that they must do (or re-do) their wills before they go. On one hand, if they've gone for years without doing this important task, two more weeks probably won't matter all that much, and the chances of dying on vacation are pretty remote. But if you need a deadline, by all means go for it – do whatever works for you to take action. Plan a vacation, and do your will. Both will be good for your soul.

Living Will/Durable Power of Attorney for Healthcare

There was a time when there was no question that your family was in charge and would take care of you if you were sick. Most likely the doctors knew your family, and so did your banker. But those times are long gone. HIPPA (Healthcare Initiative Privacy & Protection Act) formalized what used to be common sense, and while it offers you new protections, it also puts up barriers to care if all the forms aren't filled out and signed. You can thank HIPPA when you get three pages of legalese to sign every time you visit the doctor. They are required by law to be much more private and careful about what is going on with you and how you are doing... even for your closest friends and relatives.

This gives you added protection, but it also gives you added responsibility to say in advance who can and cannot know about or help you.

A living will lets you give directives as to what medical treatments you want (or specifically don't want) if you cannot speak for yourself.

Terri Schiavo is one of the most famous cases here. She collapsed in her home at just 27 years of age. After eight years of no recovery or improvement from her vegetative state, her husband took steps to have her feeding tube removed, which would cause her death. It is called a "do not resuscitate" order. Terri's parents then began to fight the order, leading to a seven-year court battle over her right to life. She didn't have a living will, so at issue was whether Terri would have wanted to live indefinitely in a vegetative state or would have preferred to die. Her parents were sure she would have felt one way, while her husband argued the opposite viewpoint. Whatever your opinion on this tragic case, a Living Will would have settled the issue without question.

This and a Durable Power of Attorney go hand-in-hand. A Durable Power of Attorney allows someone else to take care of your financial affairs if you are incapacitated. It lets the individual pay your bills, for example, or orchestrate a move for you if necessary.

Both the Living Will and Durable Power of Attorney are essential if you get sick or are injured and need assistance. As I mentioned earlier, we wouldn't have been allowed by law to care for my mother-in-law, or use her own assets to pay her bills during the last three years of her life, had these documents not been in place. Together with a will, they protect you by telling the courts who you trust to make decisions for you, and speak for you when you can't.

Have you made your appointment with your attorney yet?? $

The Happy Ending to Your Journey

Two rules for investing:

1. Preserve the principal

2. When in doubt, see rule number one.

– Warren Buffett

In a way, I feel I have told horror stories all the way through this book. Hopefully, you have realized my point has been to prevent you from making the mistakes of others, to learn from them and live a better, less stressful life.

To wrap up all the lessons I've tried to teach in your money makeover on a happier note, I want to share a story about one of my favorite clients. We started working together about five years ago, and though it has taken a bit of time, I can confidently say she is in a place where *she does not worry about her future.* She has put in place everything that she needs to make her happy *and* to be sure she will not be a burden on her sons. Believe me, this was not where we started.

46% of women consult a financial professional when making investment decisions. 38% of men do the same.

—The New Retirement Mindscope IISM Studies Commissioned by Ameriprise Financial, May 2010

When I met Mary, she had been a widow for a number of years and had two grown sons. One lives near her and the other lives out of state. She has four grandchildren. To give you some perspective, Mary lost her husband in a tragic non-work related accident. He had life insurance, so she was taken care of financially. Then her sister died. Mary inherited a bit of money from her sister, but when it came to income tax time, the CPA told her to talk to a financial planner because she had lost more than half of her inheritance to taxes.

Mary is very skittish about the stock market and any type of risk. Understandably so—it was very difficult to get her past the losses she had experienced financially. She had talked to professionals in various fields—bankers, insurance brokers and the like. No one had done anything wrong; it was that people had not really listened to her. She needed a sense of security—after all, she had lost her husband, sister and mother, all in a very short time and she felt very alone and vulnerable. Mary had financial products that were not suited for her risk level. When that happens, people want to keep money in a mattress or buried in their back yard, and a patient and caring financial advisor needs to coax them to stay ahead of inflation, or they will run out of money.

It has taken five years, but we now have Mary in a situation where she will not run out of money. I have set up income streams for her that have guarantees on them and have arranged them in five-year increments. She has long-term-care insurance, so she will not be a burden on her children. She has a life insurance policy that will last as long as she does and will leave her two sons a fair amount of money. She is currently in the process of planning her funeral. All of this did not start until she was 66 years old! I also wouldn't call her affluent.

We made quite a few changes, but I listened, went to her house for meetings and really got to know Mary. She says she doesn't worry at all about money anymore because she knows I'll take care of it. Mary trusts me implicitly and so do her sons. They all know that I have *their* best interests at heart and really care about what happens to them. My biggest rewards are that Mary says she tells me things no one else knows, she calls me "honey" and says "love you" when I leave. What could be better than that? $

To Arrive Safely...

Avoid the potholes on your financial journey:

1. Procrastination
2. Not having goals
3. Not having a plan to reach those goals
4. Lack of knowledge
5. Not having a way to measure your progress

Remember,

There is never too little and it is never too late!

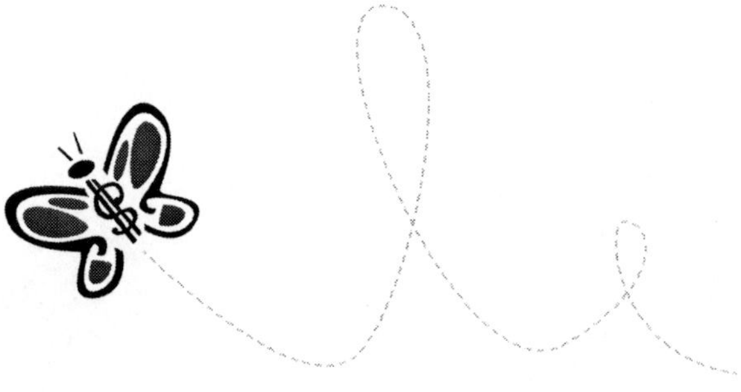

About the Author

Deborah "Deb" Schmitz

Financial Coach and Advocate,
"The Women's Money Mechanic"

Deb Schmitz brings the passion, creative thinking and analytical skills she honed in corporate research, development and management to the field of financial services, with a strong focus on women's financial health issues.

Having successfully navigated the waters of her own financial life, she became passionate about carrying the message to other women that they will be responsible for themselves, financially, at some point in their lives, and it pays to be prepared. She helps women look beyond the typical offerings of cookie-cutter financial strategies and coaches them to develop individual solutions to custom fit the unique women they are.

She works with women in all walks of life, pointing out that there's never too little, and it's never too late to create a plan.

Deb is married to Herb Helseth and is a mother of two and grandmother of three. A self-described lifelong learner, she holds both Associate's and Bachelor's degrees from the University of Cincinnati, as well as a Paralegal Certificate. She has completed the NASD Series 7, 63, and 65 Registration, and is a Certified Senior Advisor (CSA).

Her first career began at the Hilton Davis Chemical Company where she worked prior to being hired by Procter & Gamble, where she worked in research and development until taking an early retirement. During that time, she participated in the development of seven US Patents. Today, Deb lives in her dream home in East Tennessee, where she enjoys her family, golf, boating and football.

My Own Money Mechanic, Shifting Gears for a Money Makeover You Can Live With is her first book.